TABLE OF CONTENTS

CHAI TEA

HIBISCUS COCK

BUTTERNUT SQI

WATERCRESS S

DEEP FRIED PR

PRAWN COCKT/

SCALLOP WITH CHORIZO AND BROAD BEANS   15

SCOTCH EGGS   17

THAI RICE NOODLE SALAD   19

PASSION FRUIT PUMPKIN   21

APPLE VINEGAR PICKLED LOTUS ROOT   23

HONEY PICKLED CHERRY TOMATOES   25

HEIRLOOM TOMATO CAPRESE GARLIC BREAD   27

QUICHE - BLACK OLIVE, TOMATO, SPINACH   29

FIG-LICIOUS GOAT CHEESE MOUSSE SANDWICH   31

ARNOLD BENNETT OMELETTE   33

RAMEN NOODLE SOUP   35

TURKEY & CHESTNUT PASTRY   37

WILD MUSHROOM RISOTTO   39

SEAFOOD PASTA   41

OX CHEEK PIE   43

SALMON GRAVLAX PLATTER   45

LAMB KOFTA   47

FIVE FRUIT HARVEST ROAST PORK BELLY   49

PAELLA:CHICKEN, PRAWN AND CHORIZO   51

LEMON TART   53

ELDERFLOWER PANNA COTTA WITH BERRIES   55

STEWED PEAR WITH OSMANTHUS AND JUJUBE   57

LAVENDER & STRAWBERRY SHORTCAKES   59

EIGHT TREASURE RICE PUDDING   61

ILLUSTRATE YOUR OWN FAVORITE RECIPE HERE!   63

CHAI TEA

8 CARDAMOM PODS

1 CINNAMON STICK

2 CLOVES

3 PIECES OF FRESH GINGER

2 STAR ANISES

FULL FAT MILK
2 1/2 CUPS

1 1/2 CUPS WATER

2 TBS ASSAM TEA LEAVES

3 TBS DEMERARA SUGAR

1. PUT ALL THE INGREDIENTS APART FROM TEA LEAVES INTO A BIG SAUCEPAN.

2. BRING IT TO BOIL THEN ADD TEA LEAVES AND SIMMER FOR 1 HOUR AND 15 MINUTES.

3. PASS THE TEA WITH A FINE SIFTER AND SERVE IN A TEA CUP OR MUG.

FOR HIBISCUS SYRUP:
500G CUP GRANULATED SUGAR   200G DRIED HIBISCUS FLOWERS
500ML WATER
METHOD:
PLACE ALL THE INGREDIENTS INTO A SMALL SAUCEPAN, BRING TO
A BOIL. SIMMER FOR 20 MINUTES AND LEAVE IT TO COOL DOWN.
STRAIN THE SYRUP THROUGH A SIEVE. RESERVE SOME FLOWERS

FOR COCKTAIL:
SOME ICE, SOME LEMON-LIME SODA(FOR EXAMPLE 7-UP)
SQUEEZE OF LIME JUICE, SOME RASPBERRIES, 30ML HIBISCUS SODA,
70ML VODKA , SOME LIME SLICES
METHOD:
MIX EVERYTHING TOGETHER AND POUR INTO A NICE GLASS.

HIBISCUS COCKTAIL

INGREDIENTS

1 LARGE BUTTERNUT SQUASH
1 ONION, SLICE FINELY
1 CLOVE GARLIC, MINCE
1 APPLE, PEELED AND DICE
2 TBSP GOOD QUALITY CURRY POWDER
1 1/2 LITRE VEGETABLE STOCK OR
    CHICKEN STOCK
1 LEEK, ONLY USE THE WHITE PART
    AND THINLY SLICE IT
1 SMALL CARROT, PEEL AND SLICE
250ML FULL FAT COCONUT MILK
2 TBS BUTTER
OLIVE OIL
SOME CRISPY BACON
HANDFUL TOASTED PUMPKIN SEEDS
SOME CREME FRAICHE

METHODS

1. HEAT OVEN TO 200C. CUT THE SQUASH INTO HALF AND
   REMOVE THE SEEDS. WRAP IT IN TIN FOIL AND ROAST FOR 30
   MINUTES UNTIL IT'S SOFT.
2. USE A SPOON TO DIG OUT ALL THE MEAT AND LEAVE IT ASIDE.
3. HEAT THE BUTTER AND OLIVE OIL IN A BIG STOCK POT. TURN
   THE STOVE TO LOWEST HEAT AND ADD CURRY POWDER FIRST
   AND WAIT FOR 20 SECONDS UNTIL THE AROMA COMES OUT.
4. SAUTE ONION, GARLIC, LEEK AND CARROT FOR 3-4 MINUTES
   UNTIL IT'S SOFT AND THE FRAGRANCE COMES OUT.
5. STIR IN APPLE AND FRY FOR A FUTHER 2-3 MINUTES. ADD
   BUTTERNUT SQUASH, STOCK AND COCONUT MILK. BOIL IT
   FIRST THEN SIMMER FOR 1 - 1 1/2 HOURS.
6. USE A BLENDER TO BLITZ THE SOUP AND RETURN TO THE POT TO
   REHEAT. SEASON WITH SALT AND PEPPER.
7. GARNISH WITH CREME FRAICHE, PUMPKIN SEEDS AND CRISPY
   BACON. READY TO SERVE!

Butternut Squash and Coconut Soup

WATERCRESS SOUP

WITH PANCETTA LARDONS AND BOILED EGGS

INGREDIENTS:

4 LARGE BUNCHES WATERCRESS, RESERVE SOME NICE LEAVES FOR GARNISH. WASH THOROUGHLY.

3 LARGE POTATO, PEELED AND THINLY SLICED.

30G BUTTER

OLIVE OIL

1 ONION, THIN SLICE

1 LEEK, ONLY USE WHITE PART AND THINLY SLICE

3 CLOVES GARLIC

2 LITRE VEGETABLE STOCK

SOME COOKED PANCETTA LARDONS

SOME BOILED EGGS

DOUBLE CREAM OR CREME FRAICHE

METHODS:

1. HEAT UP BUTTER AND OLIVE OIL IN A BIG SOUP POT AND SAUTE ONION, LEEK AND GARLIC UNTIL IT SMELLS NICE AND HAS A SOFT TEXTURE.

2. ADD POTATO INTO THE POT AND KEEP FRYING FOR ANOTHER COUPLE MINUTES.

3. ADD VEGETABLE STOCK IN THE POT AND TURN THE STOVE TO THE STRONGEST POWER TO BOIL IT FIRST THEN TURN DOWN THE POWER TO THE LOWEST AND SIMMER FOR ONE AND HALF HOURS.

4. CHECK THE POTATO IS ALL NICE AND SOFT AND TURN OFF THE FIRE. LEAVE IT FOR 10 MINUTES TO COOL DOWN A LITTLE BIT THEN ADD WATERCRESS INTO THE POT. GIVE IT A QUICK STIR.

5. USE A FOOD PROCESSOR TO QUICKLY PUREE THE SOUP. SEASON IT WITH SALT AND PEPPER.

6. POUR THE SOUP INTO A BOWL OR SOUP PLATE. GARNISH WITH CRISPY PANCETTA LARDONS, BOILED EGGS, WATERCRESS AND A DRIZZLE OF DOUBLE CREAM OR CREME FRAICHE.

LIV WAN ILLUSTRATION

Deep Fried Prawn Balls with Almond Flakes

Procedures:

1. Use a food processor to process the fatty pork first. Process the pork until it looks like fine mince.
2. Add the prawns to the mix and process for a further 1-2 minutes. Move everything into a big bowl once the prawns and mince are finely minced.
3. Add all the seasonings, onion and spring onion. Mix the mixture clock wise for 3-5 minutes.
4. Roughly chop the almond flakes and spread onto a plate. This way the almond is smaller and easier to stick to the prawn balls.
5. Wet both hands with cold water and take a little bit of mixture and roll it into a ball. Repeat this procedures until all the mixture has been rolled into balls.
6. Coat the prawn balls with almond flakes.
7. Heat up the oil in a wok and fry the prawn balls at the lowest heat for 3-4 minutes. Moving the prawn balls around gently will help the prawn balls keep a nice round shape.
After 3-4 minutes turn the stove to the highest temperature and fry the balls until they turned to a nice golden colour.

Ingredients:

380g prawn, peeled
120g fatty pork, small diced
75g onion, finely chopped
1 tbs of spring onions, finely chopped
150g almond flakes
Half tbs potato starch or corn flour
1 egg white
Oil for fried the prawn balls 600ml

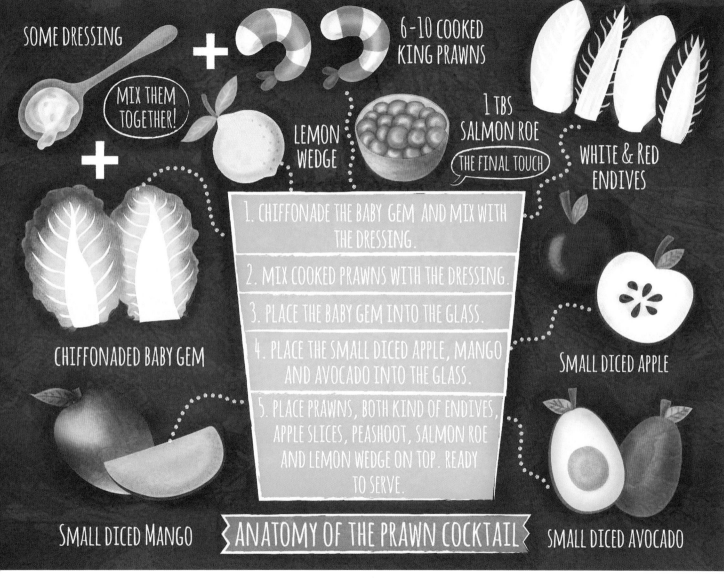

SOME DRESSING

MIX THEM TOGETHER!

6-10 COOKED KING PRAWNS

LEMON WEDGE

1 TBS SALMON ROE

THE FINAL TOUCH

WHITE & RED ENDIVES

CHIFFONADED BABY GEM

1. CHIFFONADE THE BABY GEM AND MIX WITH THE DRESSING.

2. MIX COOKED PRAWNS WITH THE DRESSING.

3. PLACE THE BABY GEM INTO THE GLASS.

4. PLACE THE SMALL DICED APPLE, MANGO AND AVOCADO INTO THE GLASS.

5. PLACE PRAWNS, BOTH KIND OF ENDIVES, APPLE SLICES, PEASHOOT, SALMON ROE AND LEMON WEDGE ON TOP. READY TO SERVE.

SMALL DICED APPLE

Small diced Mango

ANATOMY OF THE PRAWN COCKTAIL

SMALL DICED AVOCADO

Scallop with Chorizo and Broad Beans

Ingredients:

Small handful
Broad Beans

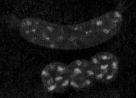

Small handful
Diced Chorizo

30ml
White wine

A squeeze of
lemon juice

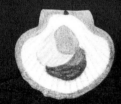

4 Large
Scallop with roe

1 Tbs
Butter

Procedures:

1. Remove skin of chorizo and dice it. Remove the shells of broad beans.
2. Heat up butter in a small sauce pan, add chorizo and fry for a couple minutes.
3. Add broad beans, white wine and lemon juice, reduce down until nearly dry, season with salt and pepper.
4. Heat up some oil in a frying pan and cook scallops. Season with salt and pepper.
5. Place chorizo and broad beans on to a scallop shell and 2 scallops per portion.
6. Garnish with some salad.

SCOTCH EGG

850G GOOD QUALITY
SAUSAGE MEAT

10 LARGE EGGS
8 BEATEN

2 TBS PARSLEY
CHOPPED FINELY

2 TBS CHIVE
CHOPPED FINELY

200G PANKO
BREAD CRUMBS

1 TBS ENGLISH
MUSTARD

1/4 TBSP
CAYENNE PEPPER

PLAIN FLOUR
FOR DUSTING

PERFECT DISH FOR PICNIC

1. TAKE A DEEP SAUCE PAN, EIGHT EGGS AND ADD ENOUGH WATER TO COVER THE EGGS.
2. BRING TO BOIL AND SIMMER FOR 3-4 MINUTES. GENTLY TURN THE EGGS THROUGHOUT AS THIS WILL HELP THE YOLK STAY CENTRAL. IMMEDIATELY COOL UNDER WATER AND PEEL ONCE COOKED.
3. MIX SAUSAGE MEAT, PARSLEY, CHIVE, ENGLISH MUSTARD AND CAYENNE PEPPER IN A BIG BOWL THOROUGHLY. SEASON WITH SALT AND PEPPER.
4. DIVIDE STEP 4 INTO 8 BALLS, FLATTEN MIXTURE INTO PATTIES AND PUT EGG IN THE MIDDLE AND GENTLY SHAPE THE MEAT AROUND THE EGG. PUT FLOUR ON YOUR HANDS TO MAKE THIS EASIER.
5. PREPARE 3 PLATES, ONE FOR BEATEN EGGS, ONE FOR FLOUR AND ONE FOR THE PANKO BREAD CRUMBS.
6. COAT THE SCOTCH EGG WITH FLOUR FIRST THEN EGG THEN EGG THEN BREAD CRUMBS. PREHEAT OIL IN A DEEP PAN TO 170C AND FRY THE EGGS FOR 4-5 MINUTES. GENTLY TURN THEM WHILE COOKING.
7. ONCE THEY ARE GOLDEN AND CRISPY THEY ARE READY TO SERVE.

How to make dressing?

CHILLI
FINELY CHOPPED
+
CORIANDER
FINELY CHOPPED
+
GINGER
FINELY CHOPPED
+
SPRING ONION
FINELY CHOPPED
+
SPRING ONION
FINELY CHOPPED

LIME
ZEST AND JUICE
+

MIX ALL OF THE INGREDIENTS FOR MAKING THE DRESSING IN A BOWL.

2 TBS FISH SAUCE

1/4 TBS SALT

1 TBS LIGHT SOY SAUCE

+

1 TBS WATER

1 TBS SUGAR

LEAVE DRESSING AT LEAST 30 MINUTES BEFORE USE.

Thai Rice Noodle Salad

10-12 CHERRY TOMATOES CUT INTO HALF

500G MUSSELS WASH AND STEAM

250G RICE NOODLE BLANCH

150G PRAWN PEEL AND BLANCH

200G SQUID CLEAN. CROSS-CUT AND BLANCH IT

Passion Fruit Pumpkin

INGREDIENTS:
1 PUMPKIN
2~3 PASSION FRUITS
1 TBS SALT
1 TBS SUGAR

SEASONINGS:
2~3 TBS SUGAR
(ADJUST TO SUIT)
1/2 TBSP SALT

METHODS:

1. THINLY SLICE THE PUMPKIN.
2. MIX PUMKIN WITH 1 TBS SALT AND SUGAR, LEAVE IT TO MARINADE FOR AT LEAST A COUPLE HOURS.
3. WASH THE PUMPKIN WITH COLD WATER AND DRAIN IT PROPERLY.
4. SEASON PUMPKIN WITH PASSION FRUIT JUICE, SUGAR AND SALT.
5. KEEP IT IN THE FRIDGE FOR 24 HOURS AND READY TO SERVE!

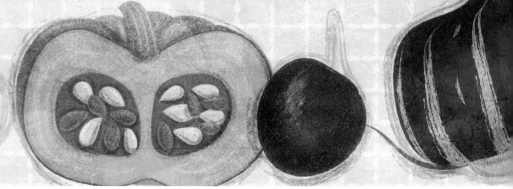

Apple Vinegar Pickled Lotus Root

1/2 CUP APPLE VINEGAR

WASH AND PEEL THE LOTUS ROOT AND THINLY SLICE IT.

1 LEMON JUICE AND ZEST

APPLE VINEGAR

POUR INTO THE JAR

400G LOTUS ROOT

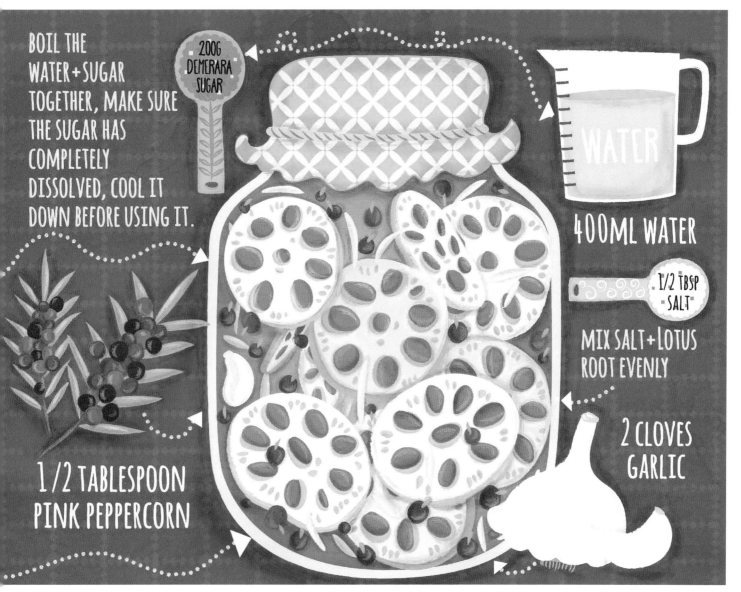

BOIL THE WATER + SUGAR TOGETHER, MAKE SURE THE SUGAR HAS COMPLETELY DISSOLVED, COOL IT DOWN BEFORE USING IT.

200G DEMERARA SUGAR

400ML WATER

1/2 TBSP SALT

MIX SALT + LOTUS ROOT EVENLY

2 CLOVES GARLIC

1/2 TABLESPOON PINK PEPPERCORN

HONEY PICKLED CHERRY TOMATOES

300ML RICE VINEGAR

VINEGAR

BOIL

300ML WATER

WATER

10 CHINESE SALTED PLUMS

"BOIL VINEGAR, WATER, HONEY AND PLUMS TOGETHER IN A POT AND LEAVE IT TO COOL DOWN BEFORE USE IT"

350ML HONEY

HONEY

"PEEL CHERRY TOMATOES FIRST AND THEN PLACE INTO THE JAR"

"POUR THE HONEY VINEGAR WATER INTO THE JAR"

450G RED CHERRY TOMATOES

450G YELLOW CHERRY TOMATOES

"MARINADE FOR 12 HOURS, READY TO SERVE!"

HEIRLOOM TOMATO CAPRESE GARLIC BREAD

INGREDIENTS:

2 LOAFS CIABATTA BREAD, HORIZONTALLY CUT IN HALF
4 TABLESPOONS SALTED BUTTER
1 TABLESPOON PARSLEY, FINELY CHOPPED
2 CLOVES OF GARLIC, MINCED
SQUEEZE OF LEMON JUICE
250G MOZZARELLA CHEESE, SLICE 1CM THICK
3-4 DIFFERENT TYPES OF HEIRLOOM TOMATOES, SLICE 0.5CN THICK
SEA SALT

METHODS:

1. MIX BUTTER, PARSLEY, GARLIC LEMON JUICE EVENLY AND SEASON WITH SALT AND PEPPER.
2. SPREAD THE BUTTER ON THE BREAD AND PLACE THE CHEESE ON THE BREAD. PRE-HEAT THE OVEN TO 200C. BAKE IT IN THE OVEN UNTIL THE CHEESE STARTS TO MELT. TAKE IT OUT OF OVEN.
3. PLACE THE HEIRLOOM TOMATO ON THE TOP AND SPRINKEL SOME SEA SALT ON TOP FOR SEASONING.

Quiche

BLACK OLIVE ♥ TOMATO ♥ SPINACH

INGREDIENTS:
450G HOMEMADE QUICHE PASTRY
1 POTATO, PEELED
1 BUNCH SPINACH
HANDFUL BACON LARDON
1 EGG
120G MILK
10G GRATED PARMESAN CHEESE
PINCH SALT
PINCH GROUND WHITE PEPPER
HANDFUL SHREDDED CHEDDAR CHEESE
HANDFUL BLACK OLIVE, THIN SLICED
HANDFUL CHERRY TOMATO, PEELED AND CUT INTO HALF
8" PIE TIN

PROCESS:

1. LAY THE PASTRY IN THE PIE TIN AND GET RIDE OF ANY EXCESS PASTRY AND LEAVE IT IN FRIDGE FOR 30 MINUTES.

2. PRE-HEAT OVEN TO 200C. TAKE OUT THE PIE PASTRY FROM FRIDGE AND USE A FORK GENTLY STAB SOME HOLES IN IT.

3. PUT A SHEET OF BAKING PAPER AND SOME BAKING BEANS ON THE PASTRY, THEN BAKE FOR 20 MINUTES.

4. AFTER 20 MINUTES, REMOVE BAKING PAPER AND BAKING BEANS. BRUSH A LAYER OF EGG WHITE ON THE PASTRY, THEN BAKE FOR 8-10 MINUTES UNTIL THE PASTRY HAS A NICE COLOUR.

5. THINLY SLICE CHICKEN BREAST AND MARINADE WITH 1 TBSP RICE WINE, PINCH OF GROUND WHITE PEPPER. LEAVE IT FOR 10 MINUTES AND STIR FRY IT WITH BACON LARDON.

6. THINLY SLICE POTATO AND STIRY FRY IT.

7. BOIL WATER WITH 1TSP OIL, BLANCH THE SPINACH INCLUDING STALKS AND COOL IT DOWN UNDER COLD RUNNING WATER. SQUEEZE THE WATER FROM THE SPINACH AND ROUGHLY CHOP.

8. MIX EGG, MILK, SALT AND PEPPER EVENLY AND SIFT IT.

9. PUT THE INGREDIENTS INTO THE QUICHE PASTRY AND FILL THE PASTRY WITH EGG AND MILK MIXTURE. ONLY FILL THE PASTRY TO ABOUT 90 PER CENT FULL JUST IN CASE THE FILLING OVERFLOWS DURING BAKING

10. PRE-HEAT OVEN TO 200C

11. SPRINKLE PARMESAN CHEESE AND CHEDDAR CHEESE ON TOP AND BAKE FOR 35 MINUTES. READY TO SERVE.

FIG-LICIOUS!
GOAT CHEESE MOUSSE ♥ OPEN-FACED SANDWICH

INGREDIENTS:
1 LOAF BREAD
SOME CRUSHED PECANS
SOME FRESH FIGS
GOAT CHEESE MOUSSE
SOME THYME LEAVES
SOME HONEY
FOR MOUSSE:
200G GOAT CHEESE
150ML MILK
50ML DOULBE CREAM

PROCESS FOR MOUSSE:
1. USE A STAND MIXER TO MIX GOAT CHEESE AND MILK TOGETHER UNTIL SMOOTH.
2. WHIP THE DOUBLE CREAM AND GENTLY FOLD IT IN THE GOAT CHEESE WITH A SPATULA. SEASON WITH SALT AND PEPPER.

PROCESS FOR SANDWICH:
1. SLICE AND TOAST BREAD AND SPREAD A LAYER OF GOAT CHEESE MOUSSE.
2. SLICE FIGS AND PUT ON TOP OF THE MOUSSE.
3. SPRINKLE SOME THYME LEAVES, CRUSHED PECAN AND DRIZZLE SOME HONEY ON TOP. READY TO SERVE!

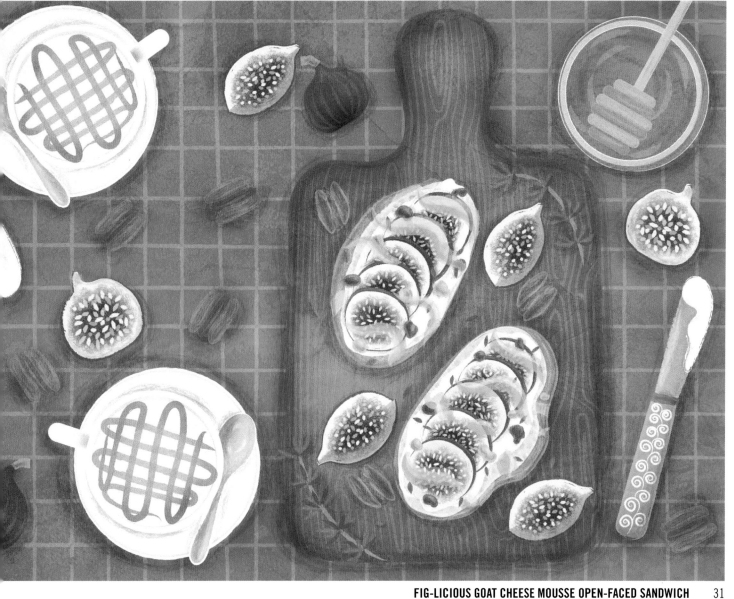

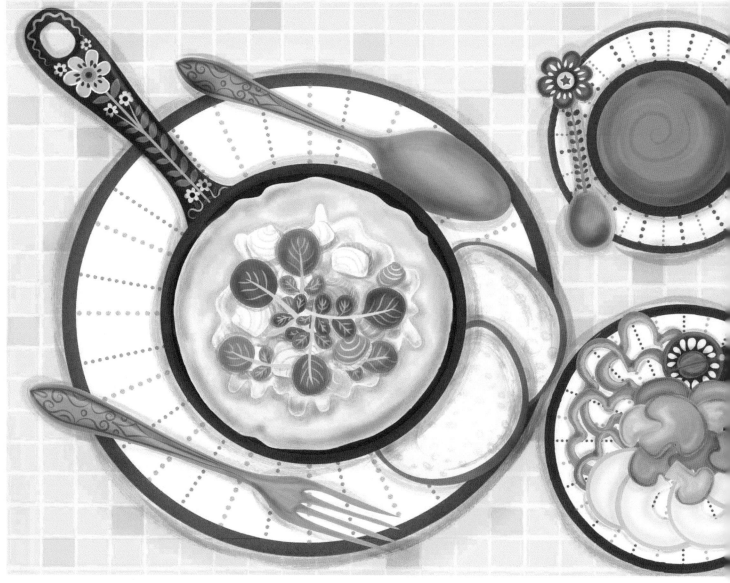

ARNOLD BENNETT OMELETTE

INGREDIENTS:

250G BONELESS AND SKINLESS SMOKED
    HADDOCK FILLET
400ML DOUBLE CREAM
1 SHALLOT, CHOP FINELY
1/2 CUP WHITE WINE
1/2 TBSP ENGLISH MUSTARD
1/2 CUP GRATED GRUYERE
2 EGGS PER PORTION/PERSON FOR OMELETTE
HANDFUL WATERCRESS FOR GARNISH

A DELICIOUS OPEN-FACED OMELETTE NAMED
AFTER THE FAMOUS ENGLISH WRITER "ARNOLD
BENNETT". I LEARNED THIS DISH WHILE
WORKING IN A RESTAURANT AND HAVE COOKED
IT MANY TIMES FOR MY FAMILY AND THEY LOVE
THIS DISH WHICH COULD BE SERVED AS A
STARTER, LIGHT LUNCH OR BREAKFAST. I
USUALLY PREPARE A DECENT AMOUNT OF
SAUCE AND KEEP IT IN THE FRIDGE FOR 3-4
DAYS SO I CAN EASILY ENJOY THIS DISH OFTEN.

METHODS:

1. CUT THE SMOKED HADDOCK INTO 2CM DICE.
2. HEAT SOME OLIVE OIL IN A SAUCE PAN AND SAUTE THE
   SHALLOTS UNTIL SOFT.
3. ADD WHITE WINE AND REDUCE DOWN TO 1/3.
4. ADD DOUBLE CREAM AND ENGLISH MUSTARD. REDUCE DOWN
   TO 3/4 AND STIR IN GRUYERE CHESE.
5. KEEP STIR THE SAUCE UNTIL GRUYERE CHEESE HAS
   COMPELETELY MELTED THEN ADD SMOKED HADDOCK.
6. COOK FOR FURTHURE 2-3 MINUTES, SEASON WITH SALT AND
   PEPPER AND TURN OFF THE FIRE.
7. BEAT 2 EGGS AND SEASON WITH SALT AND PEPPER
8. HEAT SOME OIL IN A SMALL FRYING PAN. ADD EGGS, LEAVE IT
   FOR 10-15 SECONDS AND USE A FORK TO GENTLY STIR IT A
   LITTLE BIT. REMOVE FROM STOVE.
8. PUT 1 TBS SMOKED HADDOCK SAUCE ON THE TOP OF STEP 7
   AND PUT IT INTO OVEN (200C) COOK ABOUT 7 MINUTES UNTIL
   THE SAUCE START GETTING GOLDEN BROWN COLOUR.
9. GARNISH WITH WATERCRESS ON TOP. READY TO SERVE.

Ramen Noodle Soup

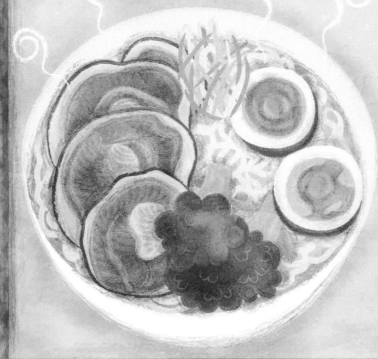

Ingredients for Ramen:
(Serving 2)

400ml Stock
200g Ramen
2 Spring Onions, julienne it for garnish
Handful of Broccoli or any other kind of vegetable
1 tbs White miso

Ingredients for stewed eggs and pork:

2 Eggs
1.5 kg Pork belly, remove the skin
1 Onion
2 Spring Onion

Methods for Stew Eggs and Pork:

1. Season the pork belly with ground black pepper and salt then roll it and tie it up with string
2. Boil the eggs in boiling water for 6 minutes, cool down immediately and peel them
3. Sear the pork in a frying pan and place it in a stock pot, add all the ingredeints apart from eggs in the stock pork. Boil first then simmer for 2-3 hours until the pork is tender.
4. Leave to cool down, add the eggs and store the dish in the fridge overnight.

Methods for Ramen:

1. Blanch the broccoli, heat up the stock and cook ramen noodle in the boil water.
2. Remove the egg from the pot and leave it aside, heat up the pork and slice it.
3. Stir in 1 tbsp of white miso into the hot stock, season the stock with salt and pepper before serving
4. Place ramen noodle in a big bowl then pour hot stock into the bowl. Place sliced pork, spring onion, stewed eggs and broccoli on the top. Ready to serve.

おいしいです

Turkey & Chestnut Pastry

SMALL HANDFUL COOKED CHESTNUT FINELY CHOPPED

250G ROAST TURKEY FINELY CHOPPED

2 CLOVES GARLIC FINELY CHOPPED

1 SHALLOT FINELY CHOPPED

1 SMALL BUNCH SPINACH

1 TBS THYME LEAVES

1 PACK PUFF PASTRY

1 EGG, BEATEN, USE FOR EGG WASH

ANOTHER DELICIOUS WAY OF USING UP LEFTOVER TURKEY OR CHICKEN!

1. BLANCH SPINACH AND WASH UNDER COLD WATER. SQUEEZE ANY EXCESS WATER OUT.

2. HEAT SOME OIL IN A FRYING PAN. FRY GARLIC AND SHALLOTS ONLY UNTIL SOFT.

3. ADD TURKEY AND FRY FOR 1 MINUTE. ADD CHESTNUT, THYME LEAVES AND COOK FOR ANOTHER 2-3 MINUTES. SEASON WITH SALT AND PEPPER. DRAIN ANY EXCESS LIQUID AND LEAVE ASIDE TO COOL DOWN FOR LATER.

4. ROLL OUT PASTRY ON A FLOURED BOARD AND USE A RING CUTTER (12CM) TO CUT OUT THE ROUND SHAPES IN THE PASTRY.

5. BRUSH SOME EGG ON THE EDGE OF THE ROUND PASTRY AND PUT 1TBS OF STEP 3 MIXTURE INTHE MIDDLE.

6. FOLD INTO HALF MOON SHAPE AND USE A FORK TO PRESS DOWN THE EDGES TO SECURE THE MIXTURE. BRUSH A LAYER OF EGG ON THE SURFACE OF THE PASTRY. PRE HEAT OVEN TO 200C AND BAKE FOR 20-25 MINUTES UNTIL THE PASTRY IS GOLDEN AND CRSIPY. READY TO SERVE!

INGREDIENTS:

1.5 LITER CHICKEN/VEGETALBE STOCK
1 HANDFUL OF DRIED PORCINI MUSHROOMS
2 SHALLOTS FINELY CHOPPED
3 CLOVES GARLIC FINELY CHOPPED
400G RISOTTO RICE
75ML WHITE WINE
4 LARGE HANDFULS OF MIXED MUSHROOMS, SLICE
HANDFUL GRATED PARMESAN CHEESE
FEW SPRIGS FRESH THYME
1 TBS BUTTER
SALT AND PEPPER

PROCEDURES:

1. SOAK RICE IN THE WATER
2. HEAT UP SOME OIL IN A DEEP PAN AND FRY THE SHALLOT AND GARLIC TOGETHER
3. SOAK PORCINI MUSHROOM IN WARM WATER FOR 15 MINUTES
4. POUR WHITE WINE INTO PAN AND COOK UNTIL THE RICE IS NEARLY DRY
5. ADD THE PORCINI MUSHROOM INTO THE RICE
6. POUR ENOUGH STOCK INTO THE PAN TO COVER THE RICE, LEAVE IT TO SIMMER
7. KEEP AN EYE ON THE RICE AND KEEP IT TOPPED UP WITH STOCK IF IT'S DRIED UP
8. ADD REST OF THE MUSHROOMS TO THE PAN
9. ADD BUTTER, PARMESAN CHEESE AND SEASON WITH SALT AND PEPPER WHEN THE RICE IS NEARLY COOKED
10. SPRINKLE SOME CHOPPED FRESH THYME OR PARSLY AND IT'S READY TO SERVE!

WILD
MUSHROOM RISOTTO

THYME

P S

PARMESAN

WHITE WINE

INGREDIENTS:
1. 2 SHALLOTS, FINELY CHOPPED
2. 500ML DOUBLE CREAM
3. 400G FRESH LINGUINE PASTA
4. 1/2 BOTTLE GOOD WHITE WINE
5. HANDFUL DILL
6. 200G BROWN CRAB MEAT
7. 200G WHITE CRAB MEAT
8. 480G FRESH PRAWN, PEEL
9. LEMON FOR SERVE
10. SALT AND GROUND PEPPER

PROCEDURES:

1. HEAT UP A COUPLE TABLESPOONS OF OIL IN A DEEP PAN AND FRY THE CHOPPED SHALLOTS UNTIL SOFT.
2. POUR WHITE WINE INTO THE PAN REDUCE DOWN TO HALF
3. ADD CREAM INTO THE PAN AND REDUCE DOWN BY 3/4. STIR IN BROWN CRAB FIRST AND COOK FOR AFURTHER 30 SECONDS. ADD THE WHITE CRAB MEAT
4. ADD PRAWNS INTO THE PAN AND BRING TO THE BOIL
5. SEASON WITH SALT AND GROUND PEPPER. GARNISH WITH CHOPPED DILL AND A LEMON WEDGE. THE DISH IS READY TO SERVE WITH COOKED LIGUINE PASTA.

PLAIN FLOUR

2 TBS, SEASONED WITH 1 TBS SEA SALT

150G SMOKED BACON LADONS

3 OX CHEEKS, CUT IN HALF

3 BAY LEAVES

GROUND PEPPER

Ox Cheek Pie

1 PACKET

3 TBS TOMATO PUREE

1. PREHEAT THE OVEN TO 150C. HEAT SOME OIL IN A FLAMEPROOF CASSROLE POT.
2. ROLL THE OX CHEEKS IN THE SEASONED FLOUR, THEN FRY THE CHEEK IN THE CASSEROLE POT. COOK UNTIL WELL BROWNED.
3. REMOVE THE MEAT AND SET ASIDE. ADD THE BACON AND FRY UNTIL LIGHTLY COLOURED. ADD THE ONIONS, BAY LEAVES AND COOK UNTIL ONIONS ARE SOFT. STIR IN GARLIC AND THEN TOMATO PUREE. STIR OCCASIONALLY UNTIL THE PUREE STARTS TO CATCH THE POT.
4. ADD WINE AND THYME, THEN RETURN THE MEAT TO THE CASSEROLE POT. BRING IT TO SIMMER. COVER WITH GREASEPROOF PAPER AND THEN THE LID COVERING THE PAPER AND MEAT. COOK UNTIL THE CHEEKS ARE TENDER SEASON WITH SALT AND PAPPER.
5. SERVE WITH SOME GREEN VEGETABLE AND COOKED PUFF PASTRY.

1 BOTTLE RED WINE

RED WINE

SEA SALT

6 CLOVES GARLIC

HANDFUL THYME LEAVES

2 ONION

Salmon Gravlax Platter

450g fresh salmon with skin on
1 bunch fresh dill chopped
2 tbs sea salt
1 tbs sugar
1 tbsp peppercorn toasted and crashed
1/2 lemon's juice
1 lemon zest
1/2 tbsp ground coriander or fennel seed
2 tbsps vodka

1. Rinse salmon under cold water and pat dry with kitchen napkins.

2. Mix the sea salt, sugar, crashed peppercorn and ground coriander in a bowl evenly.

Serve with all your favourite condiments

3. Mix vodka and lemon juice together

4. Lay couple sheets of cling film on a tray and put salmon on the middle of tray. Pour vodka and lemon juice on salmon.

5. Sprinkle lemon zest on the salmon and then sea salt and spice mixture evenly on salmon.

7. springkle dill on the salmon and wrap salmon nice and tight with cling film.

8. Try to find something heavy put on top of salmon.

9. leave it in the fridge for 3 days and take it out. Wash away the sea salt and herb. Slice very thin to serve.

Lamb Kofta
WITH TZATZIKI AND PITTA BREAD

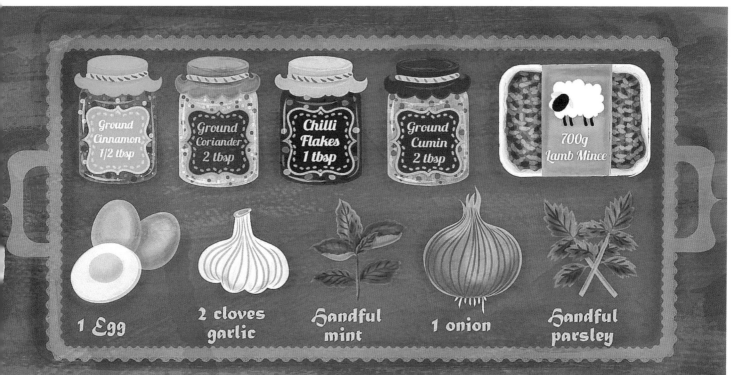

Ground Cinnamon 1/2 tbsp

Ground Coriander 2 tbsp

Chilli Flakes 1 tbsp

Ground Cumin 2 tbsp

700g Lamb Mince

1 Egg

2 cloves garlic

Handful mint

1 onion

Handful parsley

1. SOAK THE WOOD OR BAMBOO SKEWERS IN COLD WATER FOR 30 MINUTES.
2. CHOP GARLIC, MINT, ONION AND PARSLEY FINELY. ADD ALL THE INGREDIENTS INTO A BIG BOWL.
3. MIX THE INGREDIENTS EVENLY AND KEEP MIXING FOR 2-3 MINUTES. SEASONION IT WITH SALT AND PEPPER.
4. WET YOUR HANDS AND SCOOP SMALL AMOUNT OF THE MIXTURE AND SHAPE INTO OVAL SHAPED LOGS AND SKEWER IT.
5. CHARGRILL EACH SIDE FOR 3-4 MINUTES AND READY TO SERVE!

Five Fruit Harvest Roast Pork Belly

INGREDIENTS:

3 APPLES, CUT INTO HALF
1.5 KG PORK BELLY
2 ONIONS, CUT INTO HALF
HANDFUL THYME
1 BOTTLE BULMER'S FIVE FRUIT HARVEST CIDER

MARINADE:

2 TBS THYME LEAVES
4 TBS DEMERARA SUGAR
2 TBSP SALT
1/4 TBSP GROUND BLACK PEPPER
COUPLE PINCHES GROUND CLOVES

PROCEDURES:

1. MARINADE THE PORK BELLY OVER NIGHT
2. PUT THYME, ONION AND APPLE IN A BAKING TRAY. THEN PLACE PORK BELLY ON TOP
3. POUR THE CIDER INTO THE TRAY AND IT SHOULD COVER MOST OF THE PORK BELLY BUT DON'T SOAK THE SKIN.
4. PRE-HEAT THE OVEN TO 200C
5. COVER THE TRAY WITH A LAYER OF BAKING PAPER THEN TIN FOIL
6. ROAST THE PORK BELLY FOR 3 HOURS KEEP CHECKING THE LIQUID IN THE TRAY. IF THE LIQUID DRIES OUT TOP UP WITH SOME WATER
7. REMOVE TIN FOIL AND BAKING PAPER ONCE PORK IS SOFT. KEEP COOKING UNTIL THE CRACKLING IS CRISPY. READY TO SERVE!

Paella

CHICKEN, PRAWN AND CHORIZO

400G Paella Rice

OLIVE OIL

150G BROAD BEANS

2 CLOVES OF GARLIC

1 RED PEPPER

1 ONION

1 LITRE OF CHICKEN STOCK

1 TSP PARSLEY FINELY CHOPPED

200G PEELED PRAWN

1 TSP TOMATO PUREE

400G SKINLESS CHICKEN THIGH FILLETS

60G CHORIZO

1 1/2 TBSP SMOKED PAPARIKA

PAPARIKA

1. CHOP THE GARLIC, ONION AND CARROT FINELY, THEN SLICE THE CHORIZO AND DICE THE CHICKEN THIGHS.

2. PUT SOME OIL INTO A PAELLA PAN, ADD GARLIC, ONION, CARROT AND CHORIZO. FRY UNTIL THE ONION IS SOFT AND ADD CHICKEN AND PAPRIKA, THEN FRY UNTIL THE CHICKEN HAS TURNED TO A GOLDEN BROWN COLOUR.

3. STIR IN THE TOMATO PUREE THEN ADD RICE AND STIR FOR A COUPLE MINUTES. ADD 1 LITRE OF BOILING CHICKEN STOCK, SALT AND PEPPER.

4. COVER THE LID AND BRING TO THE BOIL, THEN SIMMER UNTIL THE RICE IS NEARLY COOKED AND STIR IN BROAD BEANS AND PRAWNS.

5. SPRINKLE CHOPPED PARSLEY ON TOP AND GARNISH WITH LEMON WEDGES.

1 CARROT

Lemon Tart Filling:

170g Caster Sugar

120ml Double Cream

4 Eggs

40ml Lemon juice
2 Lemon zest

Procedures:

1. Use a whisk to mix eggs and sugar until the sugar is dissolved.
2. Add rest of ingredients into the bowl and give it a good mix.
3. Preheat the oven to 160c.
4. Fill the tart filling into the cooked tart pastry in a tart tin.
5. Bake it for 40 minutes. Garnish with whipped cream and fruits.

Sweet Tart Pastry

375g Plain flour

250g Butter

1 Eggs

125g Caster sugar

Procedures:

1. Use a mixer to mix sugar, butter and egg until there are no lumps.
2. Add flour and mix evenly.
3. Line the pastry in the tart tin. Trim off the excess pastry.
4. Preheat oven to 160c
5. Line tart tin with foil and fill with rice or dry beans, bake for 10 minutes then discard the foil and bake for another 20 minutes.

ElderFlower Panna Cotta With Summer Berries

REDCURRANT

BLACKCURRANT

CAPE GOOSEBERRY

GOOSEBERRY

720 ML DOUBLE CREAM

180ML ELDERFLOWER CORDIAL

BOIL 1.

6 SHEETS OF GELATIN

COLD WATER 2.

180G CASTER SUGAR

SUGAR 3.

STIR IN GELATIN AND SUGAR 4.

POUR THE MIXTURE INTO THE MOULDS AND LEAVE IT IN THE FRIDGE FOR A FEW HOURS TO ALLOW IT TO SET. 5.

Stewed Pear with Osmanthus and Jujube

INGREDIENTS:
4-5 PEARS
200G ROCK SUGAR
2TBS HONEY
12 DRIED JUJUBES
700ML WATER
20G DRIED OSMANTHUS
FLOWER, RESERVE SOME FOR
GARNISH.
1 LEMON, THINLY SLICED

METHODS:
1. PEEL THE PEARS AND REMOVE THE CORES
2. BOIL THE WATER AND ADD ROCK SUGAR AND HONEY
3. ADD DRIED OSMANTHUS AND SIMMER FOR 10 MINUTES
4. GET RID OF THE DRIED OSMANTHUS FROM SYRUP
5. PUT EVERYTHING IN A BIG BOWL AND COVER WITH CLING FILM
6. STEAM IT FOR 30-40 MINUTES AND GARNISH WITH THE OSMANTHUS

INGREDIENTS

1. 500G BUTTER
2. 250G CASTER SUGAR
3. 2 TBS DRY LAVENDER FLOWER
4. 1/4 TSP LAVENDER ESSENCE
5. 125G SEMOLINA
5. 625G PLAIN FLOUR
6. 400ML DOUBLE CREAM
7. 1 VANILLA POD
8. ICING SUGAR, TO TASTE
9. 12-15 STRAWBERRIES

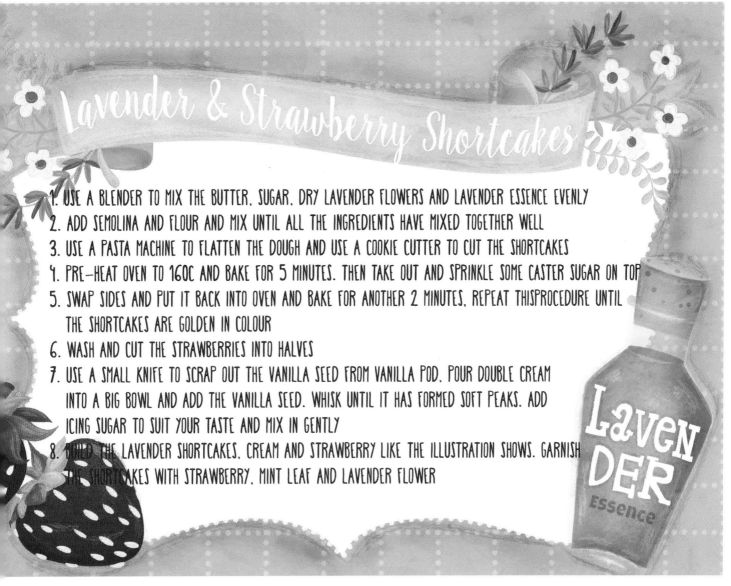

Lavender & Strawberry Shortcakes

1. USE A BLENDER TO MIX THE BUTTER, SUGAR, DRY LAVENDER FLOWERS AND LAVENDER ESSENCE EVENLY
2. ADD SEMOLINA AND FLOUR AND MIX UNTIL ALL THE INGREDIENTS HAVE MIXED TOGETHER WELL
3. USE A PASTA MACHINE TO FLATTEN THE DOUGH AND USE A COOKIE CUTTER TO CUT THE SHORTCAKES
4. PRE-HEAT OVEN TO 160C AND BAKE FOR 5 MINUTES. THEN TAKE OUT AND SPRINKLE SOME CASTER SUGAR ON TOP
5. SWAP SIDES AND PUT IT BACK INTO OVEN AND BAKE FOR ANOTHER 2 MINUTES. REPEAT THIS PROCEDURE UNTIL THE SHORTCAKES ARE GOLDEN IN COLOUR
6. WASH AND CUT THE STRAWBERRIES INTO HALVES
7. USE A SMALL KNIFE TO SCRAP OUT THE VANILLA SEED FROM VANILLA POD. POUR DOUBLE CREAM INTO A BIG BOWL AND ADD THE VANILLA SEED. WHISK UNTIL IT HAS FORMED SOFT PEAKS. ADD ICING SUGAR TO SUIT YOUR TASTE AND MIX IN GENTLY
8. BUILD THE LAVENDER SHORTCAKES, CREAM AND STRAWBERRY LIKE THE ILLUSTRATION SHOWS. GARNISH THE SHORTCAKES WITH STRAWBERRY, MINT LEAF AND LAVENDER FLOWER

INGREDIENTS:

DRIED APRICOT
1 APRICOT

BLACK RAISINS
HANDFUL

GLAZED CHEERIES
HANDFUL

SUGAR LOTUS SEED
HANDFUL

YELLOW RAISINS
HANDFUL

RED BEAN PASTE
100G

GLUTINOUS RICE
2 CUPS

PROCEDURES:

SEASONING:
1/4 TBSP SALT AND 1 TBS
SUNFLOWER OIL

SYRUP:
1 TBS SUGAR
1 TBS HONEY
1/2 CUP WATER
2 TBS POTATO STARCH WATER
(1/2 TBSP POTATO STARCH WITH 1 TBS WATER AND MIX EVENLY.)
COUPLE DROPS OF ROSE OR ANY KIND OF FLOWER ESSENCE
HONEY

1. SOAK ROUND GLUTINOUS RICE IN COLD WATER FOR 1 HOUR AT LEAST. COOK IT IN A RICE COOKER OR STEAMER. MIX THE COOKED RICE WITH SUNFLOWER OIL AND SALT WHEN IT'S STILL HOT.
2. BRUSH SOME OIL ON A MEDIUM SIZE BOWL AND CUT THE SUGAR GLASED CHERRY IN HALF. PLACE THE DRIED FRUITS AND SUGAR GLAZED CHRRIES IN THE BOWL.
3. PUT HALF OF THE COOKED GLUTINOUS IN THE BOWL AND PRESS DOWN A LITTLE BIT THEN PUT 100G RED BEAN PASTE IN THE MIDDLE.
4. USE A LITTLE BIT OF GLUTINOUS RICE TO COVER THE RED BEAN PASTE AND PLACE THE SUGAR LOTUS SEEDS AND SUGAR GLASED CHERRIES AROUND THE BOWL.
5. PUT ALL OF THE GLUTINOUS RICE IN THE BOWL AND PRESS DOWN. STEAM FOR 30 MINUTES.
6. USE A SMALL POT TO BOIL ALL THE INGREDIENTS FOR THE SYRUP. STIR IN POTATO STARCH WATER TO THICKEN THE SYRUP.
7. FLIP THE RICE PUDDING ON A PLATE AND BRUSH SYRUP ON TOP.

EIGHT TREASURE RICE PUDDING

THEY DRAW & COOK.™

The Illustrative Chef
by Liv Wan

Conceived, designed and produced
by Studio SSS and Liv Wan.

STUDIO SSS, LLC
Nate Padavick & Salli Swindell
studiosss.tumblr.com

Liv Wan
livwanillustration.com

Conversions

Common Measurement Equivalents
3 TS = 1 TBS = 1/2 FL OZ
2 TS = 1 FL OZ
4 TS = 2 FL OZ = 1/4 C
8 TBS = 4 FL OZ = 1/2 C
16 TBS = 8 FL OZ = 1 C
16 FL OZ = 2 C = 1 PT
32 FL OZ = 4 C = 2 PT = 1 QT
128 FL OZ = 16 C = 8 PT = 4 QT = 1 G

Volume
1 TS	5 ML
1 TBS	15 ML
1/4 C	59 ML
1 C	236 ML
1 PT	472 ML
1 QT	944 ML
1 G	3.8 L

Length
1 IN	2.54 CM
4 IN	10 CM
6 IN	5 CM
8 IN	20 CM
9 IN	23 CM
10 IN	25 CM
12 IN	30 CM
13 IN	33 CM

Weight/Mass
1/4 OZ	7 G
1/3 OZ	10 G
1/2 OZ	14 G
1 OZ	28 G
2 OZ	57 G
3 OZ	85 G
4 OZ	113 G
5 OZ	142 G
6 OZ	170 G
7 OZ	198 G
8 OZ	227 G
9 OZ	255 G
10 OZ	284 G
11 OZ	312 G
12 OZ	340 G
13 OZ	369 G
14 OZ	397 G
15 OZ	425 G
16 OZ	454 G

Oven Temperatures
300°F	150°C
325°F	165°C
350°F	180°C
375°F	190°C
400°F	200°C
425°F	220°C
450°F	230°C
475°F	245°C

Helpful Formulas
Tablespoons x 14.79 = Milliliters
Cups x 0.236 = Liters
Ounces x 28.35 = Grams
Degrees F − 32 x 5 ÷ 9 = Degrees C
Inches x 2.54 = Centimeters

Printed in Great Britain
by Amazon